Heart and Soul

To Barbara.
Were I a Seamus Heaney
I still could never find the words
to speak of you.

The miracle:

I am

and I am loved.

Contents

Threading the Line

Contemplating the Breath

Preface

THE JOURNEY TO BECOME A CARDIOLOGIST is long and has many legs. There are the premed days: taking high school Latin because it might help memorize the names of body parts in medical school, college courses in organic chemistry and English literature and the striving for the necessary As, and the critical medical school interviews with curveball questions. Then medical school with the first exposure to the cadaver, enigmatic and charismatic professors, and the first encounter with death. The M.D. obtained and now the stressful and exhausting internship, residency, and additional training as a cardiology fellow. Learning, learning when you know enough, learning to become independent, learning how to "read" a patient. Deciding what to do with your life, specialize? And if so, in what? And then "the career." Handling the stress of being "where the buck stops"; the agonizing questioning of self when a patient dies; the juggling of academic life, clinical life, and personal life.

All these are what these poems are about: a journey, a destination— and the realization that there was joy and fulfillment, not just in the destination but also the journey, arduous though it was.

Acknowledgements

THE AUTHOR AND PUBLISHER wish to acknowledge the following publications in which some of these poems first appeared: *Annals of Internal Medicine* ("The Joy of Medicine"); *Art House America* ("Hardening of the Arteries"); *Canadian Medical Association Journal* ("One of Us"); *CMW Journal* ("District 37"); *Cornfields, Cottonwoods, Seagulls, and Sermons: Growing Up in Nebraska;* Cascadia Press, 2017 ("District 37"); *Hippocrates Anthologies* ("Death Breakfast," "The Medical Student's First Code Blue", "The Medical Student's First IV", "Old Man and a Dog" [titled "Old Man with Hemorrhagic Stroke"]); *Journal of Medical Humanities* "To My Patients," "To Myself" [titled "Echocardiogram"]; *PACE* ("A Cardiologist Contemplates the Patient's Request"); *Wild Onions* ("Auscultation of the Heart").

TO MY PATIENTS

You gaze upon the image on the monitor
made up of bits of sound that bounce from probe
through skin to heart then back again
and think it shows what broke your heart.

But hearts are fickle things,
have reasons of their own
that you and I will never know.

TO BARB

That first year she works the 3–11,
fends off the doc who snuggles up
Your hair is beautiful.
Head nurse in recovery room
until the day their child is born
and then she stays at home
caring for the baby boy who hates to sleep
and her man exhausted from his nights on call.
She feeds him, beds him, pays the bills,
unclogs the drains and takes the car to Jiffy Lube.

In ten more years, she packs his bags
when he jets off to meetings
where he pontificates
about infarctions of the heart.
Her father introduces her as "the doctor's wife."

But when the kids grow up, she's the one
they go to when their friends won't call,
they miss the cut to make the team,
their bellies ache.
And when he wakes her up one night
I think I overate, it must be gas
she's the one who says *I'm calling 911.*
And she is right, as she is always right.

Hearing the Call

DISTRICT 37

Hard for little hands
to pump the handle fast enough
to bring the water up,
needs muscled eighth-grade boys
to do the job.

The shed out back full of coal,
hauled in by Arthur once a month.
Inside, the cast iron stove and overshoes
on every side when it has snowed.

Desks filled with spelling lists
and Frito bags. The flag up front,
the daily pledge.
The blackboard in the back.

Two shelves of books
(or were there three?).
Adventures of the Curlytops,
The Life of Jesse James.
And one with pictures
of the atria and ventricles,
the valves between.

Where would he be
without that book?
Or who'd he'd be
if there'd been one
by Yeats or Hemingway?

HARDENING OF THE ARTERIES

One evening while they're eating fried potatoes
and his mother's lettuce and mayonnaise salad,
the boy tells his folks about the new girl at school
and missing just one word on his spelling test.
And then his father says *Otto Dibbern died.*
Hardening of the arteries, they think.

It takes two hours to fall asleep.
He runs downstairs twice.
What are arteries?
and *Does hard mean like cement?*
His parents cannot help.

He'd thought when he grew up
he'd fight fires or plumb open pipes.
But when he wakes he knows
he will be something else.

JUNGLE DOCTOR

His mother wouldn't have read about Jungle Doctor
in the *Gospel Herald* or the *Grand Island Independent*
so the boy wonders where she discovered
Dr. White who fought schistosomiasis
and cut out cancers and on Sundays
preached the Word in Tanganyika,
whose books the boy devoured
like her homemade bread.
The kind of man he dreamed he'd be some day.

The first volume still stands upright
in his office at the university
between *Gray's Anatomy*
and Feigenbaum's *Principles of Echocardiography*.

JUMP SHOT

The day after Hank,
the neighbor four miles north,
brings a bull for their three heifers,
his father bolts a hoop to the side of the barn.
The boy has never watched a game
and all the father knows of sports
is hitting softballs over fences into cornfields
back in eighth grade.

He grasps the ball, heaves it up,
underhand like Wilt the Stilt.

Then in his junior year
he learns to shoot the jump shot.
Crouch down, knees bent,
hoist the ball above the head,
left hand to the side,
right hand beneath.
Jump, and raise your arms.
Release the ball.
Watch it soar towards the goal.
So sweet the swish.

But nothing like the day
he learned to torque the catheter
just above the valve
and push it down into the coronary os,
inject the dye,
then watch the vessel fill.

HANDS

The first two weeks of freshman English class
he mixes up his *d*s and *b*s
because he's taking notes with his left hand.
He'd read about a surgeon
who had saved a woman's life
by tying off a spurting artery
with her left hand.

Third year, appendix out,
a doctor lets him close the skin.
Tiny even stitches, knots all square and tight,
he's told *You have the touch.*

The final year he scrubs in
on a five-hour case. Cancer out,
the surgeon tell the resident
Sew him up. I got a plane to catch.
Tell the wife we got it all.

He ends up
pressing stethoscopes against the skin,
listening to hearts,
and holding hands
when all's been done
that can be done.

FRESHMAN HIGH SCHOOL LATIN

He stalks into his first-year Latin class,
certain he can breeze through all his notes
in half an hour the night before the tests,
finish long before the bell,
come back next day, collect his A.

Instead he finds himself standing at the board,
conjugating by the hour,
cramming for the quiz,
sweating out a B.

And in eight years, sitting ten rows up,
scribbling notes about the cranial nerves.
All the Latin he recalls is veni, vidi, vici.
Wondering: will vici ever come?

ORBICULARIS ORIS

Years before the cutting of the corpse
soaked in formaldehyde, he spends the cash
he's earned from cutting widows' lawns
to buy a plastic model of the head.

Weekends, when his friends take out their girls
to movie shows and make their moves,
he memorizes muscles of the face:

orbiculares oculi that close the lids,
orbiculares oris that pucker up the lips.

FIRST MEDICAL SCHOOL INTERVIEW

He's rehearsed a thousand times what he will say
when asked, *Why not a teacher or a CPA?*
It started with the frog heart
in my sixth grade science class, sometimes
Suffering must be wiped out.
He's memorized some Albert Schweitzer lines
to quote if they inquire about what book
he reads before he falls asleep at night.

But no one ever tells him he'll be asked
if Jonah spent three nights inside a fish.
His father was a preacher. Did they know?

He ponders *What is truth?*
before he speaks.
He doesn't know if he got in
because of what he said
or what he didn't say.

THE TELEGRAM OF ACCEPTANCE FROM
THE PRESTIGIOUS MEDICAL SCHOOL

He still recalls the angle of the sun,
the color of the sky,
the hour he tore into the envelope
from the prestigious school:
Committee pleased to offer position.

He couldn't sleep that night, remembering the C
he'd struggled for in Chemistry,
the Keats it took a month to comprehend,
the trouble grasping integrals in calculus.

Next day he tells his friends
They'd love for me to come
but the place sits in the middle of the slums.
Someone might mug my wife
when she walks home from work.

FLUNKING OUT

They borrow Cecil's truck to haul the bed,
the chest of drawers, the lamps, to Charlottesville.
His father talks about the price of corn,
Aunt Ida's broken hip, Nixon, Viet Nam.
But all the boy can think about
is learning names of nerves and arteries,
what causes heart attacks.

And then his father says
*Your mom and I will understand
if you flunk out,*

He grips the steering wheel,
stares straight ahead,
finally mutters *Thanks a lot.*

In twenty years, he drives his son
to music school in Baltimore,
tells him when he drops him off
*Your mom and I are proud of you,
know you'll end up at Julliard,*
then murmurs to himself
as he drives home
What did I say?

Finding the Vein

ANATOMY

He tells his wife over spaghetti
how he won the toss
and got to make the first slice
through the forearm skin
(anterior aspect, he emphasizes)
and how he was the one to differentiate
between the flexor digitorum superficialias
and the flexor digitorum profundis.

He remembers all the muscles
and their bony attachments
well into second year.

SOUNDS FROM THE STETHOSCOPE

Lub dub
is all he hears, first year.
In time he learns to differentiate
between the murmur of a valve that leaks
and one that doesn't open all the way.
And then he finally grasps
some sounds are loud
and innocent,
some soft
and dangerous.

THE POOL HALL

At noon some days first year
he runs across the street
to the pool hall,
rushes back in time
to sit for four more hours,
scribbling down the names
of metabolic paths
so he can pass the test.
He knows when grades
are tacked up on the wall,
his will be below
the marks of those
who ate their lunch
while poring over lecture notes,
those who never banked
the eight-ball in the side,
those who in twenty years,
will be department heads.
Doctors just like him.

FIRST CODE BLUE

First year in anatomy
he sees the fibrous patch
on the bottom of a ventricle,
scar from a heart attack.

Next year through the microscope
in pathology he visualizes myocytes
crowded out by fibroblasts
that stopped a woman's heart.

And then, third year,
through the stethoscope,
he hears the lub-dub stop.
The room fills up with doctors, nurses,
paper strips running out the little box
that monitors the heart.
They tell him
Push the breastbone down,
further down, faster, faster.
Do not stop

but in half an hour they do,
pull up the sheet,
tell the nurse *Go get his wife.*

NIGHT CALL

Some nights first year
his wife is wakened by him thumping on her back.
Percussing out your lungs, I guess.
They taught us yesterday
he mumbles when she asks.

That terrible intern year,
he rushes from his call room cot,
yells out *Is that VTach in 409?*
The nurses laugh
Go back to bed, we never paged.

Now what wakens him at night
is what rouses up old men.
When back asleep,
he dreams of ringing phones,
racing through deserted streets,
stenting open arteries,
then nodding off
on the sagging sofa
in the doctors' lounge
waiting for his morning rounds.

WHITE COAT

First week, first year,
he gets his coat.
He stuffs the pockets
with the reflex hammer
and the tuning fork
he's taught to twang,
then press against a toe.
Tongue depressors, rubber gloves,
a tube of Vaseline,
cards to test for occult blood,
of course his stethoscope.
Spots of red on both the sleeves
he never can bleach out.

He washes, starches, irons the coat the night before
he steps into a room first time
and says *Hello, I'm student doctor so-and-so,*
glad it hides his pounding heart.

POT CASE

Their first day of pathology, they go into the lab
and find the pots resting on tabletops,
canopic jars of hearts and lungs
and other vital parts. Their job:
to find what killed the people in the pots.

That night, he tells his wife
he was the one to spot
the ruptured gut. She asks
Did she have kids? How did she make ends meet?
We are not told such things, he says.

WHY HE BECAME A CARDIOLOGIST

At a party a lady asks him why
he decided to become a cardiologist.
He throws out a line or two, thinks he's said enough,
but the woman sets down her glass of pinot
and says *I really want to know.*

He talks about the QTc—if it is less than 0.45
he can assure his patient
she will not die of *Torsades de pointes,*
that if the pulmonary capillary wedge is less than five
the dyspnea's not cardiac.
She rolls her eyes. *You should have been a CPA.*

So he mentions sarcomeres and myosin,
the Starling curve, procainamide.
Words I've never heard.

But then he finally says
It must have been that second year
when that professor strode into the lecture hall
and talked of jolting fibrillating ventricles
and Christmas cards from should-be widows every year.

STUDENT DOCTOR NURSE

After passing pharmacology second year
they can work as nurses,
and so he does, twice a month.
He's taught to roll the patient side to side
when changing soiled sheets,
shown how to know pills have gone down
instead of staying stuck
between the gums and cheek,
and when to stay and when to leave
when the doctor
comes into the room
and pulls up a chair.

DR. CRAMPTON

They spend the last half of second year,
dissecting dendrites in the brain,
isolating tumor cells
or, in his case, poring over charts
of people who dropped dead.
Find out his mentor said.
Was it the heart or something else?
He interrogates the boy every Friday afternoon.
How do you know?

He tells his wife *I can't take this anymore*
but in two years, the manuscript comes out.
Two authors, his name first.

THE MEDICAL STUDENT'S FIRST IV

That first vein should have been in the farmer
kicked in the head by a cow
who never cringed when doctors pinched his leg
to see if consciousness was coming back.

But the first vein they have him stick is in a child
who just a month before was running wild,
chasing cats, eating nothing on his plate but toast with jam
and then last week told his mommy that his tummy hurt
and had a million mutilated cells in every drop of blood.

Inside the room, no nurse,
the parents watching,
thinking that he's done this thing
a hundred times before,
he wraps a band around the little arm
and swabs the site with alcohol.
Blood gushes back first stick.
He hooks the tubing up, starts the drip,
then leaves and crosses
pediatrics off his list.

FIRST DAY IN THE OR

Can't sleep
the night before
trembles through the door
dons scrubs and mask
stumbles to the sink
lathers hands
for half an hour
to be sure
is ushered in
stands fourth in line
stretches out
one arm
retracting flesh
for two whole hours
to let the surgeon
do her job
says to himself
no way in hell
they'll drag me back
when this rotation's done
and then at six p.m.
goes in alone
to see the man
back in his room
now wide awake
and hears him ask
Show me the hands
that cut my tumor out.

FIRST PATIENT ON THE THIRD YEAR
MEDICINE ROTATION

Only twenty-four. Lying in her bed
battling mutant cells pouring from her bones.
Just a month before, buying baby clothes,
her husband painting nursery walls.
His job to draw her blood,
ask about her night, listen to her heart and lungs,
tell those on rounds about her white cell counts.
Too low is bad, too high worse.

He comes back in seven years now in a long white coat.
One day he listens as a third-year clerk
tells the team about a woman,
short of breath, fluid in her legs and halfway up her lungs.
They walk into the room and there she lies,
victim of the drugs that killed the cancer cells,
and then the heart.
A picture of a little boy baking bread with mom
sits on the bedside stand.

THE EXTERNSHIP IN ETHIOPIA

Fly swatter in the operating room,
starlings roosting in rafters in the wards.
He breaks scrub during surgery
to donate a pint of blood
to the man on the table
shot at a wedding feast. Ethiopia.
A place he hopes to be in five more years.

But then one night he comes back
to their tin-roofed dirt-floored room
and finds his pregnant wife retching in the bed.
The next four weeks she loses fifteen pounds,
gags down the little that she eats,
sobs as she watches jets streaming west.

In six more years they buy a house ten minutes out.
Evenings, if his clinic's done by five,
he takes his kid to T-ball games.
At work, he tells young women
upset about their palpitating hearts
You can go back
to playing golf again.

THE MEDICAL STUDENT DELIVERS A BABY

He protests but not as vigorously as he should
when the doctors drive away that Saturday afternoon,
leaving him, the rising fourth-year,
in charge of the little hospital sixty miles from Addis.
All goes well at first. He sutures up a foot-long gash
in a man stabbed in a fight.

But then a thirty-year-old in labor
pushes and pushes for hours.
She needs forceps he is sure,
but knows they can crush the skull
and he's never wielded them before.
He orders drugs then flees the room
to find a book to help him out,
goes back to hear a baby cry,
sees the nurse cut the cord.

Help comes back at ten. They shake his hand,
nod at the mother and her child, tell him
Well done, you ought to do OB.
The nurse says not a word.

Firing the Spark

FIRST MONTH OF INTERNSHIP

After rounds he orders a CT scan for a spiculated spot
on the lungs of a woman who'd never smoked,
tells a man *We found a mass, the surgeon will come by,*
be sure to call your pastor and your wife.

Before he leaves he signs out to the one on call.
The parents of the five-year-old in 402 are coming in.
Ask them if they want their son to be a code.
Tell the woman when she wakes
about the path report.

Next Sunday when he's off, he goes to church,
walks out when a man stands up in sharing time
and tells about his totaled car.
I escaped without a scratch
but no one else survived.
Praise the Lord the preacher says.

FOUR A.M. PELVIC EXAM

It has to wait until he's seen
the other five admitted yesterday
but then reluctantly (he wants to go to bed
but knows it must be done,
it's protocol,
it's bad medicine not to do it now,
he'll be screamed at if he doesn't),
he calls the nurse and wakes the woman,
tells her *Sorry, got to do this now*,
feels for masses and adnexa,
swabs the cervix with a Q-tip,
sticks it in a vial of alcohol.

She's still awake for rounds at seven
when he tells the team about the bug
she picked up from her six-year-old
and the drugs she'll need to take,
then mentions *Oh, and by the way,
the pelvic exam was negative.*

SEX IN THE CCU

The pager beeps at eight p.m.,
the hour visitors must leave.
He answers, races to the CCU,
finds the nurses in a stew outside a bed,
curtains pulled,
listening to moans and groans.
What's up? he asks.
This woman came,
we told her he had had a heart attack,
that it was touch and go,
and then there was a code next door
that lasted half an hour—
now this.
He pulls the drapes,
finds two bodies in the bed.
What's going on? he asks.
You told me, doc,
Bed rest
for six more days.

TUESDAY MORNING DEATH BREAKFAST

On Tuesday mornings, at seven a.m.
over scrambled eggs and black coffee
he and the other residents must tell the chief
about the deaths the week before.
The plumber with the belly pain.
The seamstress who lost thirty pounds in thirty days.
The ketoacidoses.
The night before, he scours his charts.
Should he have ordered one more ECG?
Did he miss a mass?
What if he'd prescribed potassium
before he went to lunch and not at three?

After breakfast, he asks himself
why he majored in biology,
why he isn't trading Wall Street stocks.

But then he hurries to the wards
to teach his students how to listen for a gallop sound,
how to test for cerebellar signs,
how to tell a woman she has six months to live.

SIEVES AND WALLS

Now a resident, twice a month
he works an all-night ER shift.
His job: triage.
Decide who must come in,
who can go home.

One night a man's brought in by ambulance,
ashen faced, clutching at his chest.
He knows the man must stay,
pages the resident on call.
I've got a rule-out heart attack.
When she comes down in half an hour,
she finds the man now smiling, saying
Let me out of here.
If I don't get to work by seven a.m.
the boss will fire me.
Nothing wrong with him she says.
Send him out. Don't bother me.

A wall was what one tried to be,
a sieve was what they called you
if you let too many in.
But he sticks to what he said,
and in two hours' time
hears "Code Blue"
and wonders if the ambulance
would have gotten there in time
had he been a wall.

SLEEP

Rousing up
at three a.m.
to "Code Blue" pages
after half an hour of sleep

drifting off
while driving home
and waking up
across the yellow line

nodding off
while his son
played the *Pathetique*
and won.

ENCOUNTER WITH THE WOMAN
WITH A LOW BLOOD COUNT

For once all his notes are written by six p.m.
and he has signed out his ten patients
to the resident on call
and stopped by the rooms of nine to tell them
their tests were negative

except for the woman who came in the night before
with a nosebleed that would not stop.
He'd drilled out a piece of hipbone
and found no blood cells being made.
A secretary from eight to five who cleaned offices at night,
her spouse at home in bed, pills and knives locked up.

He chats about a nurse's college kid,
shoots the bull with the janitor about his Model T,
but knows the news he has to break and finally does.
She tells him as he leaves her room
Thank you, doc, for all you did.
Get out of here, it's getting late.
Go home and kiss your kids goodnight.

CARDIAC ARREST AT MONTICELLO

Ambulance run
during Easter sunrise
for a man crumbled to the ground
halfway through "The Lord is Risen."

Pressing paddles on the chest,
he charges up the joules and fires the spark,
then stands aside and watches resurrection
dance across the monitor,
sits with his Lazarus
on the shrieking journey back,
whisks him to the CCU,
then calls his wife
I'm running late, go on to church.
I've been there myself today.

SPLIT AORTA

To Dr. Ayers

No sweat presenting cases to this man
new house staff think.
A man who drawls his rs,
helps nurses move the heavy men,
says "sir" and "ma'am"
to janitors mopping the floors.

But first day on rounds an intern
tells the team
about a 22-year-old.
He broke three ribs
in a bar-room brawl.
Explains his pain.
We'll send him home today.
Ayers leads the group into the room,
asks questions no one thought to ask,
grabs a cuff,
checks the pressure in both arms,
says *Call the surgeons,*
get him prepped,
his aorta's split.

Dissection is the word we learned
the intern thinks.
It can't be that.
It was.

VITAL SIGNS

To Dr. McGuire

That first morning of internship,
after he misses the Q waves on an ECG
and can't recall that phentolamine
is the drug of choice for SVT,
McGuire takes him aside after rounds
and tells him about the first patient he saw,
thirty years before, at a big Boston hospital,
a lady with chest pain. Before he could say a word
she told him *Don't lay a hand on me young man*
until you've phoned my cardiologist.
He left the room and called. The doctor asked,
What are her vital signs? He didn't know,
ran back to check and found the woman dead.

THE DOCTOR WHO WROTE HIS NOTES IN GREEN INK

No white coat, always a suit and tie.
And no black ink, always green, from his Montblanc.
He never said where he had learned about the lungs
but by the way he glared when they'd not hear
rhonchi in an upper lobe, the residents assumed
Osler himself had taught him how to auscultate.
He'd quote verbatim articles
in journals ten years old,
tell where the authors went to school,
what kinds of cars they drove.

They swore they'd want this man to care for them
if they got sick until the day an intern
said he thought it was a fungus
caught while camping in Yosemite
that caused a patient's temperature to spike each night.
The doctor rolled his eyes
but then next day the tests came back:
Coccidioidomycosis.
The doctor stalked out of the room.

PINING FOR HIS GUNS AND HOUNDS

To Dr. Beckwith

The cardiologists who jetted around the country lecturing
about the dosing of lidocaine
for the treatment of ventricular tachycardia
had never heard of him.
He never studied the effects of digoxin
on the Frank-Starling curve in a hanging rat heart.

But there was a man from the hollow,
getting intravenous ampicillin and gentamycin
to treat the vegetations on his mitral valve,
pining for his guns and hounds.
One day Beckwith took him out for fries and a burger.
The man told everyone when he got home.

POEMS SLID UNDER THE DOOR

To Dr. Hook

Big shot head of medicine.
A man who screamed at residents
who couldn't rattle off the platelet counts,
yelled at intern wearing scrubs,
not shirt and tie, at three a.m,
snarled when they couldn't palpate engorged spleens.

Few knew about the interns who scribbled poems
on pages torn from charts
and slipped them underneath his office door
in the middle of the night,
poems he'd write long notes about,
poems about 40-year-olds with ALS,
poems about their spouses
who had packed the car
and driven home to mom.

TO CALL OR NOT TO CALL

Now a fellow,
takes call from home.

Phone rings at two a.m.
He must go in.

60-year-old,
complex arrhythmias.

Failed four drugs,
shocked fifteen times.

He wonders

does he know enough
to know what must be done?

If he doesn't,
what attending is on call?

The one who God damns every other word
before he's even heard about the case?

And if it is,
will he call him?

MOONLIGHTING

Last two years of fellowship
he moonlights in a little town
once or twice a month,
an ER doc to all
who roll in through the door—
car wrecks and heart attacks,
overdoses, broken hips.

One night he sees a three-month-old.
Won't suck and cries all night the mother says.
She doesn't know it's been eight years
since he's laid his stethoscope on any child.

Above the screams he cannot hear the lungs,
let alone the heart. At least the belly's soft.
Skin's dry. Not good. Pulse way too fast.

He searches, finds a tiny vein,
threads in a catheter, looks in a book
to find the fluid he should use,
how fast to drip it in,
then stumbles back to bed
but cannot sleep,
thinking of his one-year-old at home,
the doctor that they take her to,
who's cared for only kids for twenty years.

Before he heads back home
he calls the ward.
Heart rate's down,
the mother tells you thanks.
He hopes the pediatric doc,
if there's one in town,
will come in before her office hours.

YOU WALK TOO SLOW

To Dick Kerber

That first year in Iowa
he pages through folded paper strips
of tracings of the blips of echoed sound,
sweating. *Have I missed a flailing valve?*
Dick races in at four p.m.,
asks *Did you not see*
that twitching chordae in the ventricle?
but always in a way
he thinks, *Ah, thank you, yes.*

In another year down in Dick's lab
he tamponades the hearts of dogs,
then pushes drugs to see
if he can keep the animals alive.
It takes all day. Dick rushes in,
between a lecture and his rounds,
says *Try phentolamine*
or *Set that pump to 12 instead of ten.*
And Dick is always right.

Worried about a talk he has to give,
he asks his help. Dick listens for a minute,
cuts him off.
You know your stuff, go knock 'em dead.

On the day he leaves Dick calls him in,
says all the things one wants to hear,
shakes his hand and says
To do the things you'll have to do
as an attending doc,
you walk too slow.

Threading the Line

November, 2004

FIRST DAY AS AN ATTENDING PHYSICIAN

Last week he told
his supervising prof
about a forty-year-old.
His valve is tight,
I think he needs the knife.
But you're the boss.
Do you agree?

And now today he sees a man
and after he has listened carefully
to his story and his heart
and after he has read his ECG three times
and after he has stepped outside the room
to scrutinize yet one more time
the arteries on the TV screen,
he hesitates outside the door,
then knocks and when he's told *Come in,*
enters and tells the man
I've thought a lot about your case
and think you need three bypass grafts.
But if you like, it's always right
to check with someone else.

The man stands up, shakes his hand,
says *Thank you, doc.*
When do you want it done?

A DAY IN THE OUTPATIENT OFFICE

Eighteen on the list today.
Some did not sleep last night.
One will come at eight instead of nine
and bitch if he's not seen at once.
One two hours late will tell him
that a semi overturned,
spilling all the wheat,
blocking off the road
just like he said last year.

He reads ahead about each one,
remembers all the two a.m.'s and CCUs
and waiting rooms with weeping wives
who later smiled.
For these today,
no gurneys covered up with sheets.

Some have come for 15 years,
say *Good to see you doc*
(not enough to do, if that is true.)
Some he's glad to see.
And some, if they were all he saw,
he'd never come to work again.

When all is well
he listens twice as long
to words and hearts
and when it's not,
looks at the floor.
He talks about their weights and pressures,
levels of their bloodstream fats,
ends by saying
he will see them back next year,
always thinking
what his dad would say
about a fishing trip they'd planned

when all the corn was picked:
Lord willing.
For us both.

THREE OFFICE PATIENTS

He tells the first
Lucky for you,
swallow these drugs,
your heart is fine,
see you next year

the second
Lucky for you,
a week from now
you'll have a new aortic valve.
See you in three months

and the third
No catheters or pills for you.
That trip you said
you'd take to Italy some day?
Now is the time.

LUNCH

At parties, when he goes,
if people find out who he is
they ask *What kind of doc are you?*
and then *Where do you work?*
And if he cannot get away,
they ask the little things
(they think) like
When do you eat lunch—at 12 or one?
It all depends, he says,
thinking how just yesterday
the last one on his morning list came late.
Said she'd had a fainting spell the night before,
hit her head, fell back asleep,
No I didn't called an ambulance.
Took two pills to thin her blood instead of one,
for a couple days at least.
He sends her for a CT scan (by now it's almost one,)
and then the nurse knocks on the door.
We added on the man who called at ten,
he said you told him he should come
if anything was wrong.

THE NOON OVERBOOK

He works her in at noon—
she's demanded she be seen.
The pain goes down her arm.
He nods when told
she ran the Boston Marathon last week,
(34th place for her age.)
He doesn't raise an eyebrow
when she says she's had 12 caths,)
has the secretary get her records faxed
while he listens with his stethoscope
(it's now a quarter after one,)
then tells her *Your heart is fine,*
shakes her hand and walks her out the door,
then races back to see his one o'clock,
and overhears her tell the clerks
You won't see me again,
that quack who calls himself a cardiologist
just said it's not my heart.

THE CLEVELAND CAVALIERS

He's seen her every May for twenty years,
walked her through her heart attack,
heard how she visits shut-ins twice a week,
smiles when she rattles on about the squirrels
robbing cardinals of their seed.
He doesn't call with lab results after eight.

And then the other day the nurse out front
says she's here six months ahead of time.
He asks *What's wrong?*
*Last night my heart was pounding in my chest
and skipping beats.*
*Did you forget to take your pills,
drink three cups of coffee in the afternoon,
think you heard a burglar in the house?*
She says she doesn't know,
her mind was on her Cavaliers
who lost in triple overtime at one a.m.

STRESSES IN THE OFFICE

She's gained ten pounds. No time to exercise,
back to smoking cigarettes. He groans—
up all night stenting open arteries,
lecturing at noon to second-years (missed lunch,)
meeting with the boss at two about productivity—
and then he hears her say
she's finally gotten custody of the twins
(the daughter's serving time,)
they're still not sitting up at 13 months.

ALL HE NEEDS TO HEAR

They wonder why he asks about the pizza and chips,
why he wants to know
if they must stop to catch their breath
when hauling out the trash,
if they take their pills at night,
if they make it to the gym
three times a week.

They cannot wait for him to listen
through his stethoscope because they're sure
the sounds that travel through the tubes
tell him all he needs to hear.

A ROUTINE CATH

He slips the tube through the vessel wall
like he's done a thousand times before,
advances it until it dives into the artery,
injects the dye so he can see
if there are blockages
and then the man yells out
Damn pain is back.

The pressure drops.
He pushes epi, shocks the heart
twenty times.

He finds the wife.
She asks him *Why?*

Day after day
he ponders,
over dinner,
at the barber,
in his bed.
Should I have used another catheter?
Should I have pulled it back a quarter inch?
Not pushed the dye so fast?
Should I have slept an extra hour the night before?
When will the lawyer call?
Should I have gone to business school instead?

ROUNDS

The team of nine waits patiently for him.
Three new third-year clerks,
peering round to see how stethoscopes are worn.
Three interns, one unshaved
(a code at five, respiratory arrest at six,
high potassiums, orders for sleeping pills all night.)
Two residents, a fellow, halfway through her final year,
who thinks she knows what's best,
but when she pushes for a patient to be cathed
and she is wrong, he waits to talk to her alone
when rounds are done.

Eight a.m. Six admitted overnight,
12 others to be seen. No empty beds,
folks stretchered in the ER halls.
Paged four times since he got in.
Can anyone go home?

First patient indisposed
so they go next door. The intern rattles on
Get to the point or we'll be here 'til five
he thinks but interjects an Osler quote,
then asks him *Did you hear a gallop sound?*
He listens to the heart and lungs,
agrees with plans for tests and blood
and leads the queue back to the bedpan room.
He hears about her labs and night
and tells her *Home today.*
And so it goes for three more hours.

See you back at four he says,
then heads back to the wards himself.
The man in 301 had nodded
when the intern said his valve was tight
but didn't have a clue
and so he grabs a chair and draws a diagram

that would have flunked him back in second grade
but now the man nods his head.

And then the daughter of the mother with V-Tach
who wouldn't listen to the resident.
She likes his graying hair.

Then the tests the patients had endured:
echoes, arteries lit by dye, x-rays,
scans of chambers left and right.
Some he reads himself, some he can't.
Can he trust what someone else has said?

It's sit-down rounds at four.
He hears the stories of the day,
routine to him, aware it is not so
for those who got the needles,
were stuck for half an hour
inside claustrophobic tubes,
got boluses of drugs,
(*This won't hurt—oh yeah!*)
those waiting, waiting for the news.
They make a list of who
will go to whom to tell that news:
what will be done next day,
what can't be done, and why.
The hardest ones he sees himself.
He closes doors, tries to figure out
How do you say what is not good?
How would someone
tell his mother what he has to say?

He leaves at six, forgets to turn on Second Street.
Did someone check the lytes before
they gave the second Lasix dose?
At dinner doesn't hear
the saga of his son's stolen base
Did we send the man in 403 home too soon?

Finally falls asleep,
dreams of a heart attack he missed.

AUSCULTATION OF THE HEART

He tries not to listen too long
because even if all sounds normal
the patient will think he heard
the whish of a leaking valve about to let go
and loose blood to flood her lungs.

But if he doesn't listen long enough
she will think that by spending less time on her,
he can see more patients
and make more money,
and buy a yacht?

While listening
should he look at his stethoscope
or off at the wall of brochures
about how to lose weight and stop smoking?
Or should he close his eyes?
Should he smile
(but not too much)?
Surely, he must not frown.
Should he nod his head?
Surely, he must not shake it.

His right hand presses the stethoscope
against her chest.
What should he do with his left hand?
Can he lay it on her shoulder?
Or should it hang down limp and loose?

At least he need not fear
that she knows what he thinks.
He thinks.

DELIVERING BAD NEWS

He's listened to her heart and lungs,
peered into her ears and nose each June
for twenty years; he doesn't need to read
his notes about her broken hip in '99
and heart attack five years ago because
he can recall it all. He knows she owns
the parlor on the square,
laughs when she talks about the colors
that the teenage girls dye their hair.

But today he'll have to tell her
that her marrow's packed with tumor cells.
He ponders as he pauses at the door.
Do I tell the news at once
or should I ask "How was your day?"
Should I say "They've found a lesion in your bone"
or should I use the cancer *word?*
Will she ask about her odds?
If she doesn't, should I tell her anyway?
When she leaves, should I shake her hand,
or will she want a hug?

He knows tonight she'll tell the news
to someone else and that no matter how he tried
he may have told it wrong.

THE OLD MAN AND THE DOG

They page from Emergency and he rushes there
to find the old man weak as a lamb on the left
and strong as a lion on the right,
saying garbage when he meant garage.
Sad, but glad I put him on the pill
to stop the clots from breaking from his heart
and rushing to the head he thinks. *I tried.*

But then his CT scan comes back
Blood bursting out of arteries has caused the stroke.
Blood that leaked because he took the pill.
The pill the man had said *God damn I'll never take*
because his dad had bled out on that pill.
But he, the doctor, told the man
You should take the pill.
The man had said *You are the doc.*

And now he smiles and shakes the doctor's hand
and says, *You are the dog.*

Note: Doctors prescribe blood thinners for many patients with atrial
fibrillation, hoping to reduce the chance of a blood clot, originating in the
heart, being expelled and blocking off a brain artery and causing a stroke.
The risk of bleeding from the blood thinner is higher than the risk of a
stroke if the patient does not take the blood thinner.

WAITING FOR THE SPEAKER

Waiting in the lecture hall
three hundred miles from home,
he thinks *I have the time.*
Should I call and check that patient's CT scan?
Afraid that if he does
he'll find out what he feared,
and then what should he do?
Wait to phone until he's back
or call and hope he gets the answering machine
and he can tell himself *I tried*?
A man about to take a ten-day cruise
to celebrate his golden wedding anniversary.

CONDOLENCE NOTES

He writes them to the widows of his patients
who thought they had indigestion and tried Pepcid
or fought blockages for twenty years before they lost.
But today there is no card to send.
No spouse, no child.
No list of contacts in the chart,
no numbers scotch-taped to the fridge.
The neighbors called the cops.
Three days of papers
piled up at her door.

THE CLUB

As they walk out from the Brahms concert
his wife nudges him and says,
That's Louise, she's in my book club.
That must be her husband.
Before he can say anything, she beckons to her,
and in twenty minutes
the four of them are having coffee.

He and Ben chat about the Eagles and the mayor,
and then when Ben discovers he's a physician,
Medicare and HMOs.
Ben looks at cancer cells
instead of sonograms of hearts,
grew up in the Bronx, not on a farm.

But they both know they belong to the same club
whose members have nightmares
about images they thought were innocent.

WHO HE WILL TELL TODAY

The one
afraid of doctors, pills,
and ICUs,

the one who thinks
she is the only one
who's ever had a heart attack,

the one who says
no way they'll poke
a needle in my wrist

he'll tell
about the catheter snaked up his arm
the stent they stuck
into his widow-maker artery.

THE DOCTOR UNDERGOES SURGERY
IN THE HOSPITAL AT WHICH HE WORKS

As they wheel him down the hall
to the operating room, staff stand aside,
whisper *There goes the doc.*
Wonder what is wrong with him?

And when the cancer has been cut away
and the anesthetic's lost its grip,
he wakes and hears on the monitors
the beeping of the other hearts
and of his own and cannot tell
which heart is his.

WHY MOM?

Fleeing some dog on the loose
because a drunk forgot to latch the gate,
she cracks her skull, breaks five ribs,
is put to bed and then a clot climbs up a leg
into a lung, and she is dead. Bad enough
if she was coming home at one a.m. from playing slots
but dear God, at noon, from mass?
And now her sons ask him,
the doctor, not the priest,
the rabbi, or the minister
Why mom?

Contemplating the Breath

CONTEMPLATING THE MINISTRY

His father and his great-grandfather
and his father-in-law
all preached the Word,
and he once contemplated the ministry
but came to find conversion of the heart
would have to do.

No poring over sacred texts,
no writing sermons late at night,
no altar calls for sinners in the pews.

Just place the paddles on the chest
and push the buttons, one to charge,
and one to fire the spark.

Sometimes he has to do it twice.
Sometimes more.
Sometimes it doesn't work.

THE CARDIOLOGIST CONTEMPLATES
THE PATIENT'S REQUEST

To Robert Frost

Kidneys, liver shutting down,
his patient begs
turn off this box
that shocks my heart if it beats too fast.

He too would choose to go with racing pulse,
not linger on until it staggers to a stop

but knows that at his end, he has no choice;
it may be fire, it may be ice.

SO SHOULD HE TELL?

Two paths, or three, at most,
they think. So should he tell
there may be five, or six, or more?

Some paths lead up, some down,
they think. So should he tell
up may be down, and down around?

He's certain of the path
they think. So should he tell
how poor the map, how blurred the print?

He knows the path that they should take,
they think. So should he tell
that he will hold their hand?

RETIREMENT PLANS

This afternoon he sits in a dark room,
watching atria and ventricles
dance across the screen and thinks
about the patient he sent last year
to fix his narrowed valve
and how, last month, the man had said
he'd run the New York Marathon again

and thinks *It wouldn't be so bad*
if the janitor finds me here tonight,
slumped forward in my chair,
head smacked against the echoes
of a beating heart.

ONE OF US

One of us asks,
Is there family?
He has two children,
a son in Omaha
and a daughter in Idaho.

One of us has her knees on his bed,
arms locked at her elbows,
caving in his breastbone an inch,
holding,
releasing,
one hundred times a minute.

One of us squeezes a blue balloon
pushing oxygen
through the tube one of us
shoved down his throat
twenty minutes ago
when he first gasped for breath.

One of us feeds him,
not meat and potatoes
as he must have been accustomed to,
but calcium and epinephrine.

We talk as if we were at a family reunion,
but not about Uncle Jack and Aunt Martha's two sets of twins,
but about blood gases and pH
and ventricular fibrillation.

One of us pushes the green button on the little machine
and waits
and then the red button.
His hands rise four inches off the bed
and then fall back.

One of us says it is time to stop.
We stop.

One of us asks what time it is
and writes it down.

One of us washes him off
like a newborn baby.

THE JOY OF MEDICINE

It's about the man
who pilgrimages to Talladega every October
because he stented the artery,
and the couple celebrating their 60th
who asked everyone to stand and clap
when he walked into the VFW hall,
and the time he was in the shower
and thought about
what the wordy lady told him in the office
the day before
and he ordered the blood test
and prescribed the right pill
and all was well
and it would not have been

and looking back now
believe it or not
it's answering the stat page
at the Little League game
in the bottom of the fifth
just as Abbie hits the ball to right field
and slides into third with a triple
and leaving the warm bed
with the candles burning
to speed to the OR
to sew up the drunk's aorta
and when he gets home
she is sleeping

but most of all
it is about the long-haul trucker
who runs to Reno twice a week
and doesn't know
he should be dead

but he does.

TO MYSELF

You gaze upon the image on the monitor.
Made up of bits of sound that bounce from probe
through skin to heart then back again
and think it shows what broke your heart.

I only wish there was a tool
I could use on me not you
to look inside not heart but soul
so I could know for what it yearns
so I could learn to make it whole.

Glossary

Adnexa: the ovaries and Fallopian tubes and the ligaments that hold the uterus in place.

Anterior: front; toward the head.

Atrium, pl. atria: one of the upper chambers of the heart that receives blood (from the lungs, left atrium; from the body, right atrium) and passes the blood into one of the ventricles.

Catheter, cath: a flexible tube passed into the body, for a cardiologist, into an artery or vein, from which it is advanced into the heart to measure pressures or to inject an agent that will outline heart structures when x-rays are taken.

Cerebellar signs: abnormalities noted on physical examination that suggest abnormal function of the cerebellum.

CHF, congestive heart failure: inability of the heart to pump an adequate supply of blood to meet the demands of the body. Symptoms may include breathlessness on exertion, awakening at night short of breath, and ankle swelling.

Chordae: rope-like structures that connect the mitral and tricuspid valves to muscles which contract to open the valves.

Cranial nerves: the nerves that exit from the brain (rather than from the spinal cord). There are twelve pairs, and they perform a variety of tasks, including carrying signals from the eyes, ears and tongue, and receiving sensation from the face.

Dendrites: extensions from nerve cells that carry electrical current and connect nerve cells.

Diurese: to urinate excessively. Generally, diuresis is caused by drugs given to remove fluid in the setting of congestive heart failure. Physicians speak of "diuresing" the patient.

Dyspnea: shortness of breath.

Epinephrine, epi: a hormone secreted by the body which increases blood pressure and heart rate. It is also a drug which can be infused in patients in cardiac arrest.

Fibrillation, fibrillate: an uncoordinated twitching of heart muscle fibers. If the left ventricle fibrillates, no blood is pumped from the heart. This is a fatal condition unless terminated with an electrical shock. Atrial fibrillation is not fatal. It may or may not cause symptoms. Clots of blood may form in part of the atria, which if dislodged, can cause strokes.

Fibroblast: a cell in scar tissue, such as the scar that forms after a heart attack.

Flexor digitorum profundus: the forearm muscle that flexes the fingers.

Flexor digitorum superficialis: the forearm muscle that flexes predominately the middle fingers.

Gallop: an abnormal low-pitched sound heard through the stethoscope in patients with congestive heart failure.

Infarct, infarction: dead tissue; the scientific name for a heart attack (death of heart muscle) is myocardial infarction.

Ketoacidosis: a condition in patients with diabetes in which the blood glucose is dangerously high; unless treated it can lead to death.

Lidocaine: a drug used to treat abnormal heart rhythms, used less often now than in the past.

Lytes: short for electrolytes; electrolytes include potassium and sodium; drawing blood to check "lytes" is commonly done.

Mets: metastasizes from a cancer.

Myocyte: a heart muscle cell.

Myosin: a protein that makes up part of the muscle.

Percuss/percussion: a part of the physical examination in which parts of the body are tapped with the fingers to determine if there is fluid, masses or air under the skin.

Os: a hole or orifice. In cardiology it refers to the origin of a coronary artery, where it arises from the aorta

Phentolamine: a drug that lowers blood pressure (rarely used) and in the past was used to stop an abnormal heart rhythm called supraventricular tachycardia (SVT).

Quinidine: a drug used to prevent abnormal heart rhythms. It is used infrequently.

Procainamide: a drug used to prevent abnormal heart rhythms.

Pulmonary capillary wedge pressure: the pressure measured with a catheter positioned in a small end-branch of the pulmonary artery. This pressure is equal to the pressure in the left atrium, which is very difficult to measure with a catheter. A low pulmonary capillary wedge pressure suggests that it is unlikely that there are problems with the heart. A high pulmonary capillary wedge pressure is often found in patients with congestive heart failure.

Q wave: an abnormal downward deflection of the electrical signal from the left ventricle of the heart, often seen in patients with a heart attack.

QTc: the time in seconds between the end of the ventricle contracting and the end of the ventricle relaxing, corrected for heart rate. It is measured on the EKG. A prolonged QTc increases the chance of dangerous fast heart rhythms such as ventricular tachycardia, and ventricular fibrillation.

Sarcomere: a part of a muscle cell. It is long and filamentous. Its stretching and contracting makes a muscle work.

Starling curve: also known as Frank-Starling Law, or Starling Law. This law says that the output of the heart depends upon how much blood enters the heart. The more that comes in, the more goes out.

SVT, supraventricular tachycardia: a fast heartbeat beginning in one of the atria. It may or may not be associated with other heart problems. Patients with SVT often have the sensation of a rapid heartbeat or palpitations. Rarely it causes the blood pressure to fall. Rarely it needs to be treated immediately with medicines or an electric shock (cardioversion).

Tamponade: an accumulation of fluid in the pericardial sac that is large enough or has accumulated quickly enough that it compresses the heart and prevents it from filling adequately. This can lead to low blood pressure and in extreme situations, death.

Torsade de pointes: a fast, dangerous, heartbeat originating in the lower chambers of the heart (ventricles). It occurs when one of the electrical intervals in the EKG, the QTc, is prolonged.

Vegetation: a growth of bacteria or fungus on a heart valve, seen in patients with endocarditis. Endocarditis is a very serious, potentially lethal infection. Strong antibiotics must be given, usually for at least several weeks.

Ventricles: the lower chambers of the heart which pump blood to the body (left ventricle) or to the lungs (right ventricle).

Ventricular tachycardia: an abnormal, usually fast, heart rhythm starting in the ventricles. Usually it is dangerous and can lead to an even more dangerous rhythm, ventricular fibrillation, which is fatal if untreated. Medicines sometimes abolish it. Sometimes an electrical shock (cardioversion) is used to terminate it.

VT: see "ventricular tachycardia."

VTach: see "ventricular tachycardia."